Tinkering
with
Texture

Jennie Rayment

Acknowledgements

An enormously huge thank you to Nick for his unfailing encouragement and support as well as more practical help such as most of the photography, proof-reading, endless envelope stuffing, parcel wrapping and pumping up my bicycle tyres. This marvellous man now copes with me in permanent residence and even loaned his pride and joy for the cover picture, he must be mad!

I am very grateful to Patsy Yardley for volunteering to check the proofs. She worked extremely hard correcting all my multitudinous mistakes and has proffered some invaluable advice. Many thanks are also extended to my father and the indomitable Shelagh Jarvis who were both press-ganged into proof reading

A huge thank you is extended to Cynthia Groves, Mary Holt, Shelagh Jarvis and Barbara Feinstein for making such superb samples. Also my thanks to Jane Bryder for all her assistance with the photocopying and to Anne Roberts from 'Out of Africa' for donating the South African material for the hanging.

Once more, a further thank you must be extended to all the students who have borne with fortitude my teaching, listened to my lectures, laughed and giggled with me, and who still come back for more. A further thank you must be extended to Tom and Diana Bishop for allowing us to photograph part of their beautiful castle. Finally, an enormous thank you to all my family for putting up with me and I send kippers from the Nutty Tart!

Copyright © Jennie Rayment 2002   ISBN 0-9524675-50
First Published April 2001
J.R. Publications
5 Queen Street, Emsworth,
Hampshire, PO10 7BJ.   Tel/Fax: +44 (0) 1243 374860 E-mail jenrayment@aol.com

Printed by Chalvington Press
Caker Stream Road, Alton, Hampshire GU34 2QA
Tel: 01420 89449 Fax: 01420 541089

International Distributors

USA & Worldwide
Quilters' Resource Inc.
P.O. Box 148850, Chicago,
Illinois 60614, U.S.A.
Tel: 773 278 5695
Fax: 773 278 1348
e-mail: info@quiltersresource.com

New Zealand
Margaret Barrett Distributors Ltd.
19 Beasley Avenue,
P.O. Box 12-034, Penrose,
Auckland, New Zealand
Tel: 64-9-525 6142
Fax: 64-9-525 6382

Contents

Tinkering with Texture   **4**

Handy Hints for the Woolpit Mafia   **5**
Useful Information   8

Floral Fantasies & More   **10**
Hexagon Ring   14
Holey Stars   16

"Tucked In" Shapes   **18**
Four "Tucked In" Squares and One Other   19
"Tucked In" Hexagons   27
"Tucked In" Triangles   30

Tuck and Scrunch   **34**
Stick and Scrunch   40

Textured Piecing   **42**
Petal Pattern Border   53

Lazy Daisy Design   **57**

Spinning Triangles   **63**

Origami Twisted Strip   **68**

Twisted Origami Hexagons   **74**

Truly Tucked Up Band   **76**

Twiddling Tucks   **81**

Wacky Wearables   **84**

Weaving for Wearables   **88**

Risqué Raiment   **94**
Gutsy Garters   99

Appendices: More Information

Going Against the Grain   **101**
Stitching Diamonds into Hexagons   **105**

Templates   **108**

Glossary & Index   **110**

Tinkering with Texture

The contents of the previous books covered diverse ways of manipulating material; this one is aimed more specifically at wall-hangings and wearables. Jazz up the jacket, zap up the vests, embellish the hangings with these uniquely novel and essentially simple natty notions. All the ideas are different from the other books and all products of my own devious explorations with one exception. It is creative play for fiddly fingers!

The first and main part of the book deals with ideas for wall-hangings and the second with ideas for wearables. Many of the techniques are interchangeable, making not only interesting garments but also intriguing wall-hangings. Why stop at garments and hangings - use the ideas absolutely anywhere from furnishings to patchwork!? In addition, **'Tinkering with Texture'** contains all the information to make the described samples. It is not necessary to purchase any of the other books.

As ever, you will see that this book is just a bit of a con trick because most of the techniques are very simple and can be done by hand as easily as on the machine. I work mainly by machine, simply for speed; it leaves more time for being down the pub! Incidentally, dear Reader, do remember that this is a book and you should not necessarily believe everything just because it is in print. It's meant to be a lighthearted and amusing, as well as being an educating and interesting workshop manual, intended for entertainment and edification. Despite any illusions, I am not the drunken, debauched, sex maniac depicted in the text - just an intoxicated, intemperate, nymphomaniac (loose-knickered lass)!

"Gentleman seeking" was the theme for my last book **'Tucked up in Bed'** and the cover picture reflected the content. This cover picture was created because a good mate of mine, Pam Watts (a splendid machine embroideress) appeared in a renowned magazine photographed alongside the helicopter she pilots in her spare time. Not to be outdone, mine was taken with the fourth man's E-type Jaguar outside the castle belonging to the chap on the cover of **'Tucked Up in Bed'**. Got to keep it all in the family!

'Tinkering with Texture' has tales of travel, sometimes steamy and sometimes just silly. In addition, there is lots of enthusiasm, odd irrelevant comments and not quite so many exclamation marks as the first book because my proof readers have objected!!!!!!!!!!!!!!!!

Did I ever think that I would write a fourth book? No. I had no notion that back in 1989 when all this started that I would end up a globe trotter, internationally known and rapidly becoming renowned for twiddling, fiddling, nipping, tucking, manipulating and manoeuvring plus a bit of sex and stitching thrown in for good measure! I have even made my American TV debut and been featured with Alex Anderson on 'Simply Quilts'.

Most Important: **The measurements in the text are given in metric and imperial. Metric measurements are not always an exact conversion of imperial. Metric seam allowances may vary for construction purposes. Select either system - do not mix.**

Handy Hints for the Woolpit Mafia

Why the title? The Woolpit Mafia are a quartet of ladies who 'terrorise' their local Quilt shop. With their leader Mistress Chris (known for some strange reason as Wendy) and her able bodied henchwoman Dot, they sally forth from Woolpit (small country village) appearing 'en masse' for classes, spending sprees, club nights etc. One is always aware of their presence as the noise level rises considerably, silence not being a Woolpit Mafia virtue. It is almost a take-over bid. Joking aside they are a smashing bunch of girls, warm hearted, kind, attentive, have an excellent sense of humour and are very bouncy! They insisted that I include some of my favourite helpful tips in the next book. I dared not refuse!

I met them all at a class some years ago. It was a new teaching venue for me and this always causes a certain amount of worry - will I do the job properly? Will the students like and enjoy what I am teaching? Will I be able to cope with the students? Will I get asked back? Most important where is the loo? There, I stood greeting the students as they came in; all was fairly peaceful as seats were found, the mountain of (mostly unnecessary but just in case) stuff unpacked, machines plugged in, then the door opened and in swept the Woolpit Mafia. A huge multicoloured tin beach bucket was plonked on their table complete with spade. Why? To hold all the rubbish of course, I presumed that the spade was to stir the garbage, dig it out afterwards or bury me. Most students usually throw it on the floor or occasionally put it in the bin provided. Obviously, this lot takes it home in buckets-full. The noise level rose dramatically and mayhem threatened. How on earth was I to control this bunch? Well I did, and what is more they keep coming back - sort of J.R. groupies.

A particular occasion stands out. One of the students, a quiet, gentle lady had arrived by train and needed a lift home. The Woolpit Mafia instantly offered a ride back with them. "Have you got a big enough car?", she asked timidly. "Yes - it's a Reliant Robin" boomed the quick reply from Mistress Wendy. (Reliant Robins are antiquated, three wheeled, unsteady vehicles, exceedingly small and the WM are not the tiniest of women). They went on at great length about the chumminess of squashing five healthy ladies into the car, how they would tie the sewing machines to the roof rack for more space, and if necessary drive with the back hatch door tied open - one of them promptly produced some string. The timid lady's face was a pallid picture, mouth dropping open and the thought of two hours or so incarcerated in the back of a Reliant Robin with this lot was horrifying. I could see the migraine coming on, so taking pity on her, I said that they were teasing, the car was amply big enough for all five of them and was most certainly not a Reliant. I didn't like to tell her it was a hearse.

For the Woolpit Mafia and others, here are some of my favourite pertinent tips and hints that may well smooth your pathway to successful fabric manipulation. Being of a particularly lazy and indolent nature, I have to confess if there is a way to cheat or an easy solution, then I will attempt to find it, (if at all possible☺).

Thread Saver: An invaluable device that saves yards and yards of thread. It is really a method of <u>continuous sewing</u>, rather like chain piecing in patchwork. (This is not my own idea - it's an old tailoring trick.)

Rummage in the trash bin and find a small scrap of unwanted fabric. At the end of any line of stitching, **DO NOT lift the presser foot, DO NOT remove the work or cut the threads but continue to sew. <u>Sew off the work on to this scrap of material. Stop on the scrap</u>.** The presser foot is now sitting on the scrap of material. Leave the scrap there - do not move it. Detach the work from the small scrap by cutting the threads immediately behind (at the back) the presser foot (between scrap and work). To continue with the next set of seams/piecing, sew off the scrap and down the next seam (scrap is now attached to the start of the work). At the end of this line of stitching, cut the scrap off from the start and sew off the main piece of work on to the scrap once again. Cut threads behind the presser foot. Repeat, repeat, repeat etc.!

This scrap is called a thread saver and will save a vast amount of thread: no long dangling ends; it prevents tangled threads in the start of the seam; threads snag less often in the bottom bobbin; the needle does not unthread inadvertently because the threads were cut too short; it's energy saving - no need to raise the presser foot; and for those who habitually deviate at the end of a seam, try using one - it may help.

Give it a whirl - it seems complicated but very easy when you get the hang of it. *Remember: the only place to cut the threads is <u>behind the presser foot</u> (once you have sewn onto the thread saver and have stopped on it).*

Threading Needles: Try wetting the needle not the thread. Lick your fingers and moisten the eye of the needle - no need to actually spit on it. Apparently capillary action helps to pull the thread through. It really does work.

Needle Down: Drop the needle into the work before engaging (lowering) presser foot. This holds the layers steady and prevents them shifting when the presser foot is lowered. When quilting, drop needle into work before turning the fabric - holds the layers steady and maintains the correct place in the seam.

For really accurate positioning of a particular seam or easing thick layers under the presser foot, drop the feed-dogs first, lower needle through all the layers, then engage the presser foot. Remember to raise the feed dogs before you commence sewing. (If the feed-dogs do not return to their full height immediately - turn the handle/fly-wheel a complete revolution.)

Tilt Table: For better vision and less neck strain, tilt your sewing machine with a thinnish book (approximately 2cm (^{3}/4") deep) or two rubber door-wedges placed under the back of the machine. Think about it - artists tilt their easels, you tilt your book, embroiderers tilt their frames, draughtsmen work on tilted tables so why don't we have a tilted machine? It gives a clearer view of the working area, especially for those wearing bi- or varifocals, and you won't hunch your shoulders quite so much.

Thread & the Machine: 1. Do not leave spare reels of thread or filled bobbins on top of the machine. Threads have a nasty habit of winding round other moving parts of the machine when you are not looking and this can lead to some terrible disasters.
2. If available, use the upright spindle and not the horizontal one. When lying horizontally, thread can catch/snag on a rough edged spool. This causes the tension mechanism to jerk and the thread can snap.
3. To prevent contrasting coloured thread showing too obviously in the stitched seam, shorten the stitch length considerably, thus linking the materials very firmly together. If the contrasting thread continues to show in the seams, colour to the correct shade with a felt tip pen (remember to touch up after washing).
4. Shredding thread can be prevented by changing the needle for a larger one (bigger eye). Needle sizes go upwards - the bigger the number, the larger the needle.
5. Incorrect stitching or tension problems are often caused by incorrect threading; if this happens re-thread both top and bottom systems totally. If you have just changed the needle check that it is the correct way round and in the correct position.

Zipper foot: Some manufacturers' zipper feet are very narrow and fit inside the feed dogs, consequently when this foot is used the outer parts of the feed dogs are redundant. There is only a very small central section of the feed dogs under the zipper foot available to pull the fabric through. To prevent the material from bunching at the start of the seam place fabric completely under the zip foot. In addition if the stitch is not quite perfect - don't panic - it is just this particular foot, the rest of the machine's performance, will still be brilliant.

Scorch Marks: Remove scorch marks with lemon juice or a weak solution of hydrogen peroxide (stuff used for lightening hair). Use a dry cloth and rub firmly. Unwashed cloth scorches more easily than washed as the dressing singes quite quickly. *There was one lass who had never ironed in her life (40+ and not ironed?). Tumble dryers and laundry services had sufficed. Briefly, I explained how to press the calico/muslin, obviously failed in my explanation because she returned, asking, "When it turns yellow - is it cooked?" How do you keep a straight face?*

Pin Trick: Try the pin trick - line up points (tops of shapes) on pin; leave pin sticking up - don't weave pin into work as normal - this may shift the points. Stitch almost to the pin, make mental note of position, remove pin and sew past.

Pinning Layers: Place all pins at **right-angles to the stitching line**, in my opinion this holds the layers flatter.

Rotary Cutters: Take apart and clean, keep fluff free. Oil the moving parts regularly. The blade will last much longer.

Invisible Thread: Use an invisible thread/nylon filament instead of your normal thread - it disguises any wobbles or anomalies in the stitching. Put invisible thread on top spool only or if really necessary in the bottom bobbin - **never** top and bottom at the same time. Use cotton, silk or any other natural fibre in the other spool, then you don't get a build up of static electricity under the presser foot which may upset the stitch mechanism. Lower the top thread tension slightly (turn dial from normal setting to a smaller number e.g. 5 to 3).

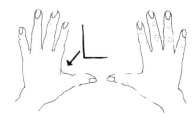

Can't tell your Left from Right?: Hold your hands out, look at the back of them. Spread your fingers out and one hand says **L - L for left**! This applies to everyone and not just right-handed people.

Seam Allowances: If your machine has a multi-position swing needle (many machines have), experiment with the needle setting to find the closest setting to your desired seam measurement. Move the needle over, further from or nearer to the inner edge of the normal straight stitch foot (with the oval/oblong slit in the top not a round hole), until the needle is set at this distance. Use this particular presser foot, then if you switch into zigzag/decorative stitch mode, the needle will not break. For most patchwork, set the needle to 0.75 cm ($^1/_4$") from right edge of presser foot.

Templates: 1. Keep your templates accurate by drawing a thick black line round the outside edge before using; if the black line diminishes (because you cut a bit off) then make another template. In addition, the template is more visible against patterned material.
2. Put a small section of double-sided sticky tape to the back of the template, peel outer protective paper off before use. The template will adhere to the material and stay correctly aligned. Replace protective paper after use - ready for the next time. *(One of my students forgot to replace the paper, absentmindedly laid the template on her chair, then sat down. Could she find it five minutes later? She rummaged around searching vainly for the lost template. None of us could tell her that it was stuck firmly to her posterior.)*

Useful Information

'Blind Hem' Stitch: This stitch is frequently used for securing the edge of a design or shape and when employed carefully gives the appearance of very neat hand stitching - people are amazed at your supposed hand sewing skills yet it was done by machine - it's a fake!

The best Blind Hem stitch pattern consists of large bite (indent) with 3/5 straight stitches in between. Many machines do this particular stitch but some machines have a variation that would suffice.

Set the machine: stitch width 1 - stitch length 1.

For current Husqvarna-Viking machines try stitch width 1.5 - stitch length 0.4.

*Some of the later Pfaff models appear to reduce stitch width to **2** only. Try this trick: activate the twin needle setting (press button), when the light shows on the twin needle setting button the stitch width is reduced by 2. Consequently if you set stitch width at **3**; press twin needle setting button - stitch width will now come out as **1**. (Neat technique for reducing the stitch width of many of the patterns but does not work for all Pfaff models.).*

Be careful, some other makes of machines display the stitch pattern, apparently set at the suggested sizes, but in reality the stitch width is wider - due to a special internal override on the stitch width setting, created by the manufacturers to prevent twin needles breaking.

Having adjusted the stitch to your desired setting, carefully sew round the edge of the rolled fold - keeping the straight stitching very close to the outside of the fold and just catch the edge of the fold with the fine 'bite' (indent). Use an 'open-toed' presser foot to enable you to see the edge of the fold more easily. Practise first!

Create an open toed foot by snapping the central bar out of the perspex appliqué foot or purchase one (available for most models). Do not use a designated Blind Hem foot (if you have one) - you are not making a blind hem but using the stitch as a method of appliqué.

Pressing Seams - to one side or open and flat?

Pressing all the seams to one edge makes the seam very bulky on that side; by pressing seams open and flat you can reduce the bulk i.e. spread the 'load'. The junction between the seams is supposedly stronger if you press everything to one side as one seam will cover the join. Sometimes this is necessary or it may be the best and fastest way to piece a particular type of patchwork e.g. Strip Patchwork.

In addition, if the seams are pressed open, it is possible to see where the next seam/stitching line should go. Depending on the type of piecing, sometimes you can see a small 'V' or maybe a triangle of a different colour in the open seam. **The next line of stitch must pass exactly through the base of the 'V' or triangle**.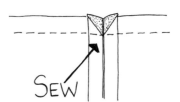

The base of these marks on the W/S will be the top of the points on the R/S and should be 0.75cm ($^{1}/_{4}$") away from raw edge, but due to inaccuracies might be different!

Have courage and sew through this junction; providing you lined up both sets of points then the join should be accurate although the seam may differ from the correct seam width. Sew through the points, do not use the designated seam allowance. In patchwork - the points should be accurate, and it is better to adjust the seam than obliterate the points.

Look inside the seam first - is there some helpful information re points/junctions?
Now, decide if you wish to press the seam open to reduce bulk or leave it pressed to one side.

Finally: Learn to love your sewing machine. It is not an ogre; it won't bite and it is far less intelligent than you are. Explore all the knobs and buttons and ***read the instruction book***. Understanding how to operate the machine will help tremendously.

Finally, finally: Remember this book is a workshop manual working through the techniques in any one chapter stage by stage. You are not supposed to leap to the end of any section <u>and guess the middle bits!</u>

Floral Fantasies & More

The one thing I really loathe about travelling is eating alone in restaurants. If you ask for a table for one, the staff invariably seat you in the centre of the room and you feel like a pariah. I much prefer slouching at the side where I can hide behind a newspaper or book and people-watch.

Picnicking in one's hotel room solves this problem and the sole disadvantage is the lack of hot food. Take-aways are a good option and lying on the bed scoffing fish and chips while watching some wonderfully ghastly TV soap is most pleasurable. But a diet of ready-prepared nosh can get most monotonous - is there another solution? Ah, most British hotel rooms have a kettle supposedly for tea and coffee-making purposes and I always travel with a heavy-duty plastic lunch box, cutlery and a tin/bottle opener. Now, what can you do with a kettle?

There are various nasty instant noodles and powdered soups, simply reconstitute for a very tasty (!) chemical cocktail, but I wanted something more substantial. Someone once told me that you can boil eggs in a kettle and yes, you can. Brown bread and butter with soft boiled eggs is one possible supper option: make sure that the egg is not cracked (makes a terrible mess inside the kettle and leaves funny floaty bits on the next cup of tea.) To get the kettle to boil for the required three minutes - leave the lid open - the kettle will continue to boil ad infinitum until you close the lid. Don't set off the fire alarm with all the extra steam - open a window first. Cans of soup can also be heated up this way: pierce small hole in can to release pressure before immersing in the kettle and heating. Remove can after a while and shake (wrap in towel, hold finger over small hole or the soup may spurt out). Replace can and continue boiling (lid off kettle) for a few more minutes.

Be careful, don't overload the circuit. Once I fused the entire second floor of a large hotel, while heating up my soup! Everything went black, not a light to be seen. Fumbling my way to the telephone to call the front desk, I didn't dare confess what I had been doing, it would have been most embarrassing! Of course, all the evidence had to be removed before the hotel maintenance man came in and caught me.

Gradually I have become more adventurous and did you know that you can have poached fish, creamed potato and petit pois all from a kettle? It is more considerate to poach the fish in your own kettle (carry a spare in the car) and just use the hotel's for the potato and peas. Place fish in cold water and bring to boil; leave in hot water. (Salmon works a treat and cooks quickly.) Place peas in other kettle, add water and boil. Petit pois will cook rapidly; when cooked drain the water onto some instant mash, add lump of butter, dash of milk and a bit of grated cheese, mix well. Open the bottle of somebody or other's Chardonnay and enjoy. The result is not cheaper than a restaurant but at least it is fresh and relatively wholesome. (If you don't like instant mash, then tinned potatoes can be added to the peas halfway through the cooking.)

PS. Rinse the hotel kettle out very well after use. I hate the thought of the next guest pouring out their morning cuppa and finding an odd pea or two floating around!

☺

Floral Fantasies

Three dimensional, three petal flowers that are ideal for embellishing, decorating and enhancing garments, hangings, quilts, cushions, boxes and baskets. Make very small ones for earrings or jewelry. How about silver and gold ones for the Christmas tree? These are textural thingamabobs, objets d'art, or if you lack a creative spirit - dust collectors.

All you need is a hexagon.

Make a hexagon template - any size will suffice (two templates on page 109). Other sizes can be constructed with a pair of compasses (instructions on page 67). Alternatively, rule parallel lines at xcm **(x")** outside or inside one of the templates from page 109; measure all six sides to check they are the same length.

The complete length of the finished flower will be approximately one third of the widest measurement of the original cut hexagon.

Select your fabric: thin fabrics such as fine silks, voiles or chiffons are ideal for very small Floral Fantasies; thicker/coarser materials can be used for larger flowers. Press material before cutting shapes - pressing shapes after cutting may distort the fibres. A light spray of starch before pressing will help to stabilise flimsy fabrics.

Lay template on fabric, draw round and cut out. Use a hard sharp pencil to mark dots in all six corners (mark on W/S). The dots should be on the stitching line i.e. 0.65 cm ($^1/_4$") from the edge (as indicated on printed templates). Easiest way - make a small hole in the template with a large pin, then enlarge the hole with a cocktail stick or thin skewer/knitting needle. (The hole has to be big enough for the pencil lead.) Once you get the hang of making Floral Fantasies, marking dots will probably become unnecessary.

Oh, I just have to digress here - 'getting the hang of it' reminds me of a lovely joke. *A newly wed cowboy arrives with his wife at the biggest poshest hotel in the area. He explained to the hotel receptionist that he had just got married that day. "Ah", she said "I expect you'll want the bridal, then". "No", replied the cowboy "I'll just hold her ears until she gets the hang of it!"* Silly but sweet.

1. Lightly pencil the relevant letter on W/S in each corner. Fold hexagon (W/S out) in half across **B/E** matching up three sides, align all raw edges. Pin right-hand sides **A/B** and **C/B** together (**A** and **C** touch). Start stitching on the dot and sew to the fold (0.65 cm ($^1/_4$") S/A). Begin exactly on the dot and not before it. 'Pickiness' pays!

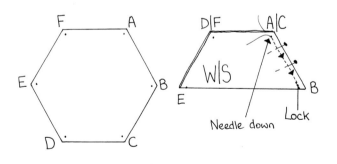

Position folded shape beneath presser foot, drop/lower needle through dot (to anchor layers), then engage (lower) presser foot and sew from dot, down seam.

Secure/lock stitching at end of seam (see next page).

Secure/lock stitches:
a. 'Reverse' sewing i.e. sew back over the stitching. **b**. Reduce stitch length considerably on reaching the end of the seam. **c**. Use stitch tie-off button or mechanism (see your instruction book for details). **d**. Lower feed dogs and stitch on the spot - run the machine slowly or the thread sometimes snaps.

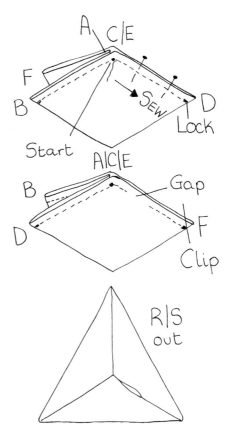

2. Fold and pin the next two sides of the hexagon **C/D** and **E/D**, (**A/C/E** touch). Turn work so that the first row of stitches is visible. Start stitching on the marked dot at **C**, sew down seam to folded edge (use 0.65 cm (¹/₄") S/A), tie-off/lock threads as described above.

3. Finally align the raw edges of the last two sides of the hexagon. Sew a short distance from the dot (by **E** where **A/C/E** touch). **Stop** stitching, raise the presser foot, leave a space/gap unsewn (approximately one third of the total seam length); complete the seam, locking stitches at end. Trim seams to reduce bulk. Carefully clip off all three corners, cut the threads across the unsewn gap. No need to press the shape. (Failing to start stitching precisely on the dot may leave a small hole at the junction of the three seams, don't panic - it can always be slipstitched later.)

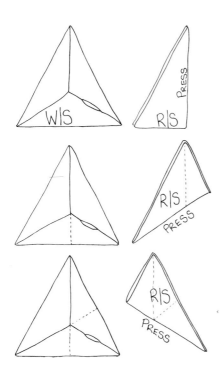

4. Turn shape R/S out through gap (diagram above), flatten out and amazingly, there is a triangle. Poke out the corners carefully; use a blunt pencil, thin knitting needle or a point turner of some sort. (Make a nifty point turner by shaving one end of a wooden lolly stick to a reasonable point - enjoy the lolly first then use the stick. Neat recycling tip for Greenies, also saves litter.) Press the shape lightly. The small hole in the seam can be left open or closed with a few hand stitches.

5. Turn triangle W/S up (seamed side) as shown in left-hand diagram. Fold one side in half and press well (R/S out); open out, fold the next side and press; finally fold last side and press. All three creases are made on the R/S and intersect at the centre of the triangle (with a bit of luck!).

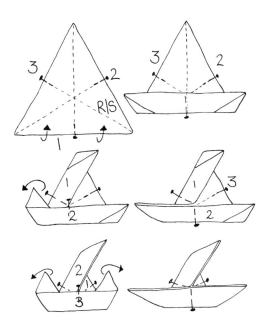

6. Lay the triangle on a flat surface with the **seamed side underneath** (if you can see the seams - it is the wrong way up!). Mark the middle of all three sides (on pressed crease) with a pin. Fold up one side of the triangle evenly and parallel to the outer edge, matching middle of side to the centre mark (where creases cross), press and pin in place after removing marker pin. Repeat with the next side; pull out the corner/flap, fold evenly and parallel. Finally, bring the last side to the centre opening out both corners/flaps, pin in place, press. All the midpoints of the three sides now touch at the central point of the triangle. Stitch across this junction (see next paragraph), carefully anchoring all the points together. Sew through all the layers.

**By hand:** start on the W/S in the centre, bring needle up through layers catching the edge of **each** fold with a **small stitch** - secure each section individually. Add a bead or button at the same time. _**By machine:**_ use a very short stitch length, sew the edges of the folds in place where they touch at the centre with the minimum number of stitches. For speed: attach the darning/hopper foot, lower feed dogs, set stitch width and length settings to zero; sew a few stitches in a sort of '**Y**' or '**T**' shape to catch all three folds together at the centre.

7. Finally, lift one 'ear' up, pull sides apart and open out, fold tip back and away from centre. Arrange to make a petal shape. Repeat with the other two 'ears' to make three petals.

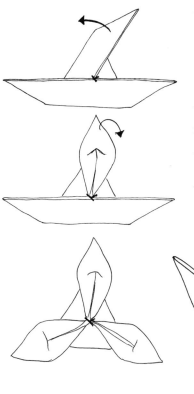

Attach the Floral Fantasy anywhere you fancy by simply sewing it on through the centre. Why not add a bead at this stage? To apply more securely, leave shape unopened at Stage 6, sew down one side of the triangle almost to the base of first 'ear' (petal), stop; twist 'ear' over and out of the way, sew up next side (leaving a small gap on the corner), and repeat with last side. Use Blind Hem stitch (page 8), small zigzag or any other decorative stitch. Rearrange the FF when sewn - petals will conceal the small gaps in the stitching. Sew the petal tips to the background fabric if you wish.

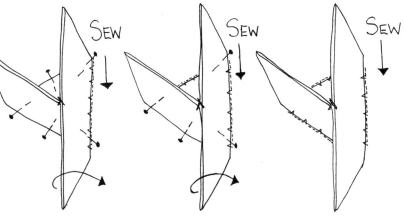

Playtime

Make lots of different sizes of Floral Fantasies and apply in random fashion to a wall hanging, or use on garments for fancy embellishment. Cover an old hat, jazz up a tired belt. Conceal any mispieced junctions on a quilt. Minuscule ones could be used as earrings. Make a bunch of flowers or use as a decorative napkin ring (colour photographs opposite page 18).

Sew two together to make a six petalled flower. How about a smaller one on top of a larger one? Create a really innovative Christmas decoration (see colour photographs oposite page 18), suspend the finished flower on a fine thread. Make a FF into a brooch/pin or stick it in your hair - attach it to a hair clip.

Try striped material for real jazzy Fantasies - the stripes will all go in different directions. Make them out of gauzes, voiles and nets and other sheer fabrics. Add sequins to the tips, and how about a tassel or two? Two FFs attached to the chest area with a tassel apiece could be a show-stopper; add small beads to the tassel ends and make 'em twirl. The mind boggles!

Experiment: try tucking folded squares into the little pockets on the petals or underneath the flower to resemble leaves; pull back and roll out the edges of the petals in other directions. Squish it, squash it and see what happens. Secure shape with a few stitches where needed.

Hexagon Ring

1. Cut six identically sized hexagons. Follow Stages 1 - 4 (pages 11 - 12), making up into triangles. Press carefully. Stitch the gap/hole in the seam by hand.

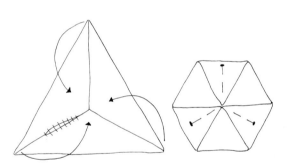

2. Lay one triangle with ***seamed side up***. Fold each of the three tips/points to the centre (where seams cross) making a hexagon, pin points in place and press well. Repeat with the other five triangles forming six hexagons in total.

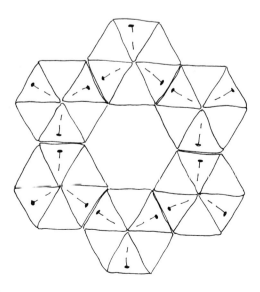

3. Arrange the six hexagons to make a ring with a hexagonal hole in the centre. Stitch ring together by sewing the relevant touching sides. ***By hand:*** put two hexagons R/Ss together, oversew or ladder-stitch the seam; continue until all six have been joined. Alternatively, experiment with other decorative stitches as feather, blanket or any faggotting type stitch. Use some of those wonderful embroidery threads for added ornamentation.

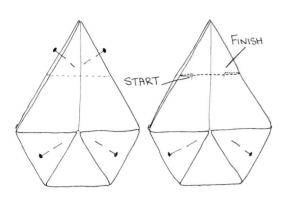

START
FINISH

By machine: take two shapes. Remove pins from one folded over tip/point on each hexagon and open out. Put the two sections back to back, align the crease and the edges of both sections, pin together, then sew along the crease. *Lower/drop needle into fabrics about 0.65cm ($^1/_4$") from edge along crease; stitch backwards to the start of the seam, sew forwards to the other side; reverse stitching 0.65cm ($^1/_4$") back along the seam. Cut threads.* (Makes a firm strong seam.) *Same stitching method can be done by hand. Wear a thimble to help push the sewing needle through all the layers.*

Continue in this fashion to link all the hexagons to make the ring, systematically unpinning the relevant folded tips/points in the correct order. It is very easy to sew the wrong sections together and that strongly stitched seam takes a fair bit of unpicking!

4. Refold the points to centre of each hexagon. Join together all three tips/points at the centre of each shape with a few small hand stitches, sew through all the layers. Add a bead, button or embroidery to both embellish and conceal the junction of all points - they may not quite touch! If machining, use the darning/hopper foot (ordinary presser foot may jam on the uneven layers), carefully sew round the tips of all three points, anchoring them securely.

5. To create more interest and extra texture to the outer edge bring the two edges of the outside folded section together, secure with a small hand stitch at the three places indicated in the diagram. Cut one more hexagon (same size as all the others), make up another Floral Fantasy flower (see previous section) and decorate the centre. Attach the flower tips to the hexagon ring (body of flower covers the hole).

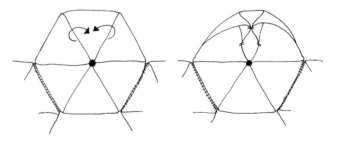

The hexagon ring looks fabulous in Christmas materials or in metallic fabrics - try Quilters' Lamé (pure Indian cotton with metallic threads woven into the fibres - easy to sew, can be pressed, available in many colours from most Quilt stores).

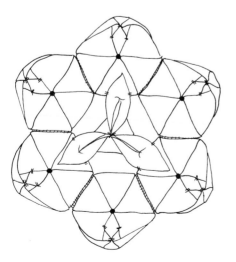

Weave ribbon through the loops under the folded tips (see colour photographs opposite page 18). Link ribbon ends together under a fold or tie a bow, trim bow ends tidily.

Decorate the ring with beads, buttons, bells and braids. Tuck silk/paper flowers into the folded loops. What about inserting small sprigs of holly or weaving ivy into the loops? (One can as ever wax lyrical about all the possibilities!) Suspend the ring by attaching a loop of tape or ribbon to the back or adhere to the wall with one of the <u>removable</u> resins/adhesives such as Blu-Tack or Pritt Sticky Buds.

Make lots of rings (leave the outer edge unrolled) and sew together for a new version of Grandmother's Flower Garden (traditional patchwork design made from hexagons).

The Hexagon Ring is double-sided and once stitched together can be used as a throw or coverlet - no need to conceal the underside. For a light lacy effect, omit the Floral Fantasies and have hexagonal holes.

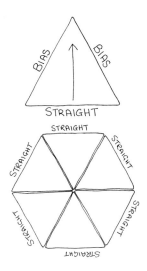

Holey Stars

1. Cut twelve equal-sized hexagons. Follow Stages 1 - 4 (pages 11 - 12) forming twelve triangles. Press carefully, close all the holes (gaps) with a few small hand stitches. Identify the straight grain side of each shape and mark it with a pin. (Every piece will have one straight grain (non-stretchy) and two bias sides (stretchy). If you can't see the grain lines, gently pull each side, the straight grained side will stretch less than the other two.)

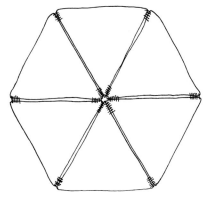

2. Form a hexagon with the straight grain edge of each triangle on the outside. All seamed sides are underneath. All shapes must butt up and lie flush. Stitch the sections together carefully and neatly where indicated in the diagram - the finished piece is reversible. Length of seam will be approximately 1cm ($^{3}/_{8}$"). Cover any gaps or holes at the centre with some form of embellishment - the good old button! **_By hand_**: slip or ladder-stitch firmly and tidily, burying all thread ends in the fabric.

By machine: use a small fine zigzag, any faggoting stitch or decorative pattern to link the sections closely; tie thread ends off or weave into the adjacent material.

3. Take the last six triangle shapes, arrange with both sets of straight grain sides butted up. Stitch in place as described in Stage 2 above. If desired, add some decoration at the junctions for extra embellishment or to cover up a glitch!

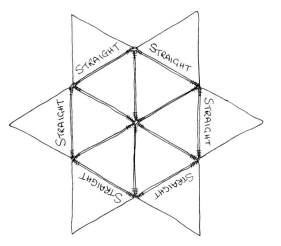

4. Roll the edges of the triangles and sew in place - the Blind Hem stitch (page 8) is a firm favourite of mine, but - perish the thought - you can always do it by hand (stitch through all the layers). The bias edges of the shapes roll more than the straight grained ones, roll edges back as far as possible before sewing down. (To prevent the fabric distorting while machining, lay a piece of paper underneath - any old sheet will suffice, no need for fancy 'Stitch 'n Tear' as the paper pulls away from the stitching afterwards. Alternatively, place some thick interfacing or craft stabiliser (Pellon - USA, pelmet Vilene - UK) on the back and trim away after stitching, or leave in place for additional stiffening). Suspend the completed star with a small loop attached to one point, or why not use as a Christmas table centre?

Be Creative - explore the potential

Embellish the inner sections of the rolled triangular shapes with machine embroidery such as vermicelli (tiny close wiggles) or any other decorative free style patterns, experiment with space-dyed or metallic threads; alternatively, use a motif from the special machine embroidery cards or even digitize a little! (Digitizing - fancy word for creative tinkering of a design/pattern on the computer. More and more sewers are now using computerised technology with astounding results.)

What about a little stuffing (nothing like it!)? Unpick the little gaps/holes on the back, push some padding in gently and re-sew the aperture (posh word for hole!).

Lay the Holey Star on some contrasting coloured sheer material, net or fine mesh, hang in the light.

Apply it to another large piece of material and use as the centre of a cushion.

What about making several of them in different sizes, then suspending for a starry mobile? How about joining lots together, rolling all the edges, to make a lacy throw, coverlet or tablecloth (see colour pictures).

Play on and enjoy!

"Tucked In" Shapes

Thinking of titles for all the new designs as well as naming the pieces of work is remarkably arduous. Should you have a funny one, a descriptive one, or some curious convoluted mishmash? sometimes my titles are really a little vomit-making such as 'Floradorable', the title of a pattern that I designed. As you will have appreciated, I adore alliteration; there is something rather splendidly rounded in the sound of a string of words all beginning with the same letter, and many of the titles reflect this passion. The title for this chapter rather prosaically describes the technique - folds are created in a particular shape and tucked inside but ....as an added bonus, they can be manipulated, manoeuvred, squished and squashed. It's just so exciting!!!!

When **'Tucked Up in Bed'** was being printed, the printer at the time referred to all my quilts and wall-hangings as rugs. No fancy titles for him, just Rug 1, Rug 2, Rug 3 and so on. It is a little upsetting to have the grand, sweated over, bled over, puzzled over and doubtless sworn over masterpiece casually dismissed as Rug 37. Somewhat takes the wind out of one's sails!

Sadly my family have picked up the same irritating habit. One morning, clutching the latest magically manipulated, exquisitely executed and dramatically diverse, creative conundrum and amazingly artistic artifact, I leapt into the bedroom. "How about this one?" A grunt, an eye opened, "Gawd, what is it - Rug 83?" OK, I agree, I suppose it was just another rug but to me it is excitingly innovative and and and.... all the other stuff! Miffed, I sneaked my cold toes under the bedcovers - if he won't take any notice of my masterpiece, he most certainly would when ten frozen lumps settled somewhere warm.

To add insult to injury, hearing the next sleepily muttered phrase "What do you do with it?" finally destroys any vestiges of a swollen head. Rug 83 is obviously a No No - yet another dust collector. Why do you have to do anything with it? Can't it just be? Surely somebody somewhere will appreciate my masterpiece. To assuage my hurt feelings, I looked up 'masterpiece' in the Thesaurus, and was directed to the art section. Now did you know that Ruskin referred to art as, "the expression of one soul talking to another"; another bozo, J. F. Millet, explained it was "a treating of the commonplace with the feeling of the sublime"; even better George Iles (don't ask who he was) referred to art as "a handicraft in flower". What could be better?

So there you are - I looked at Rug 83, (see colour photographs) my little 'handicraft in flower' with new eyes maybe it wasn't quite such a disaster after all. There is hope for me yet.

Picture: "Tucked In" Squares as described on page 22

Lazy Daisy Christmas Hanging With Floral
Fantasies: Machine pieced and quilted.
(Jennie Rayment)

Hexagon Rings and Floral Fantasies:
Machine pieced and hand finished.
(Jennie Rayment)

Christmas Table Decorations with Floral Fantasy
napkin rings and candle holder with Holey Star
table mat: Machine pieced. (Jennie Rayment)

"Tucked in" Squares (18" square): border created from same technique. Machine pieced and quilted. (Jennie Rayment)

Stripey Bag (15" x 17"): Features Tuck and Scrunch. Machine pieced and quilted. (Jennie Rayment)

Black & White "Tucked in" Squares (21" sq) decorated with Foral Fantasies. Machine pieced and quilted. (Jennie Rayment)

"Tucked In" Shapes

In this chapter, squares, hexagons and triangles are folded in a certain way, then part of the fold is tucked back in. This totally changes the original form - squares become triangles, hexagons turn into diamonds, triangles become .... read the section! As the folded edges of each shape are on the bias, the manipulative and manoeuvrable possibilities are manifold.

In my three previous books, a wide variety of textural designs have been created from various geometric forms folded in different ways. Are there any more ways to fold squares, hexagons, triangles, diamonds and rectangles? There must be many other configurations that I have not yet discovered, but here is a subtly different and innovative way - fresh from the fiddly fingers of the Muslin Mistress! An enormous quantity of different block and border designs for anything from quilts to wearables can be constructed with this new textural technique.

"Tucked In" Shapes are a doddle to produce. Simply cut the shape, press the crease, fold and tuck a bit in, twiddle! What could be easier? You can choose to work solely on the machine; do just the basic stitching by machine then complete the manipulating by hand, or do the whole design by hand. It is entirely up to you.

Use crisp and firmly woven medium-weight materials because they crease well and hold the texture. Create or restore a bit of 'body' to any thin, floppy or well-washed fabrics with a little spray starch. Starching should be done before cutting, as squirting small pieces of material with generous amounts of starch and then ironing them vigorously may result in distorted shapes.

Four "Tucked In" Squares and One Other - Finished size 20cm (8") square (exc. S/A).
S/A 0.75cm ($^1/_4$") *Metric conversion is slightly larger to make the cutting out of the shapes easier unless you really prefer to cut 21.3cm squares!*

1. Cut five 21.5cm (8$^1/_2$") squares (measurement includes S/A), these can be all the same colour. Four squares will be used for the top layer of the design and one square will be underneath (base). Take one square, fold it (R/S out) on diagonal and press the fold; open out and refold square (R/S out) on opposite diagonal, press again. Press with feeling! Try not to obliterate the first diagonal crease as you press the second diagonal one. Repeat with **three** more squares leaving **one** square unpressed. Both creases must be on the R/S of the fabric.

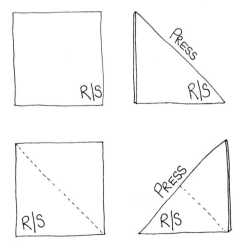

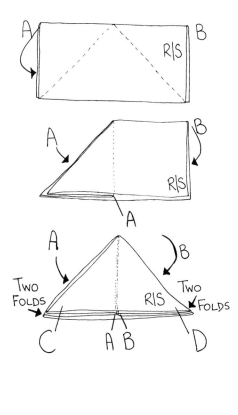

2. Fold one pressed square in half (R/S out) to form a rectangle. Lift up the top layer of the rectangle and tuck **A** corner inside. **A** folds easily inside because the fabric bends neatly on the pressed creases. Repeat with **B** corner on the other side to make a triangle. (**A** and **B** corners touch inside the folded shape.) There are now **two** folds on either side of the triangle (**C** and **D**). Line up the edges of each set of folds accurately - get the folds flush; press carefully. Make three more using the remaining three pressed squares.

3. Fold and press the last square on both diagonals; fold across opposite sides forming a rectangle, open out and press; repeat with other sides (diagram below left). The four intersecting creases resemble the crisscross lines on the Union (UK) flag. Lay square R/S up.

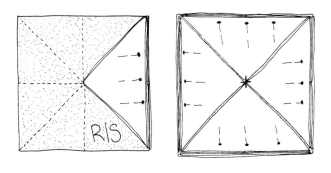

4. Fit the four folded triangles between the pressed diagonal creases; the midline of each triangle lies on a horizontal or vertical crease. The tips of all four triangles touch at the centre and all folded sides butt up. Align all outside raw edges. Pin carefully. At the centre, secure the tips of the four shapes to the square beneath with a small cross-stitch or similar. Match thread to the fabric because the cross-stitch shows.

5. Remove most pins, leaving one pin in the centre of each folded shape (on midline). Select one of the four folded triangles - each shape has two folds on either side at **C** and **D**; lift the **top** fold at **C** and bring to the centre of the shape - aligning the edge of the fold with the centre of the triangle (by the pin), part of the fold will overhang the base. Repeat with the **top** fold at **D**. Remove centre pin and tweak the folded sides until they meet evenly, lying flush in the centre of the shape along the midline at **E**. Pin all layers carefully.

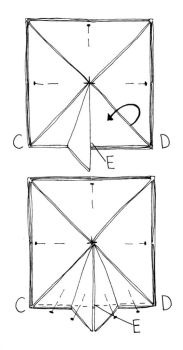

Fold the other three triangles in the same way, pinning thoroughly. Baste 0.75cm (¹/₄") inside the outer edges of the square - use longest machine stitch length. Trim the excess material level with the edge of the base square (diagram next page).

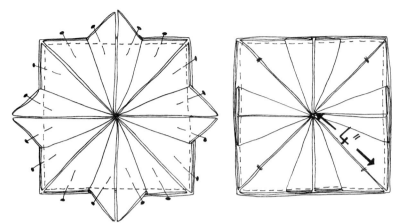

6. Working from the centre, measure 10cm **(4")** down all four diagonals, make a light mark using a hard, sharp pencil. On this mark sew both folded edges (of the adjacent triangles) to each other and to the base square.

Roll back the four sets of folds between the sewn mark and the centre point. They roll back in arcs making four petal-like shapes/spaces, pin in place as shown in **left-hand diagram below**.

Roll back the other sets of folds in the centre of each triangle above **E** and four more petal shapes appear (**right diagram**). These central folds roll out over the diagonal petals. Secure all the rolled edges with some small hand stitches or sew all the folds firmly into place by machine (Blind Hem Stitch page 8).

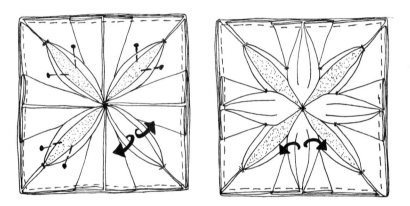

Develop the Design

Use different colours to create another dimension. Why not change the colour of the base square, then a contrasting colour will show under the four diagonal open petal shapes? Or what about inserting small pieces of extra material inside the petal shapes by **E**?

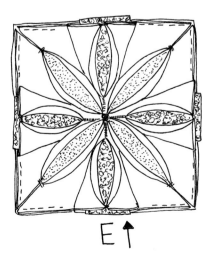

E ↑

Remove the basting along the edge by **E**, open out both folds. Cut a rough triangle of material large enough to fit the space inside these folds. Any raw edges that show after the shape has been tucked inside can be concealed by simply turning them under (to W/S), then securing with a stitch or two.

Alternatively, slipstitch part of these opened folds together from the centre to cover the top raw edge of the inserted triangular shape (see diagram).

For a subtly different appearance: At Stage 6 measure 7cm (2³/₄") from the centre down the diagonals to **F** (not 10cm/4" as previously stated). At this point anchor all the layers with a few small stitches. Remove all the basting from the outer edges. Lift the loose corners of each triangle and overlap both at **E** (centre of outside of triangle). Secure with a few stitches. Roll back the diagonal folded edges from centre to **F** making a smaller petal shape than before and revealing much more of the base square on the corners (dotted in diagram).

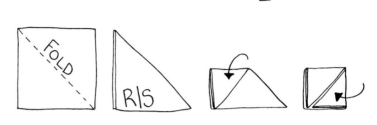

<u>Or</u> tuck another folded square underneath the other layers before stitching at F. Stitch in place.

Oh great excitement! Any size of square will suffice - if it's too big then cut a smaller one, vice versa if it is too small then cut a bigger one. (If only all one's problems could be so easily solved!) To be serious, cut four 7.5cm (**3"**) squares (one for each corner). Fold as in diagram above, basting the raw edges to prevent unfolding. Stuff/poke shape under all the layers at **F**. Sew in place, then roll the central folds of this newly inserted square to make yet another petal shape!

Finally, roll back the remaining folds as shown in the drawing above and in the photograph on page 18, to create an arced border. Enhance the centre with buttons or beads. A few Bullion or French Knots interspersed with some beads could add a touch of 'je ne sais quoi'. Embroiderers could try a Dorset button or some other decorative device. How about that ubiquitous patchwork 'bête noire' a YoYo also known as a Suffolk Puff?

The base square of fabric could be anything you fancy - try a sheer or opaque material. Why not suspend a completed panel in the window letting the light shine through the petal spaces?

Omit the base square completely, make the design on some paper (to stabilise the pieces), tear the paper away afterwards and have real holes! ('Stitch 'n Tear' could also be used but paper is more economical.)

Try - dare I say it - stripes or a directional design, the result is fantastic. For the most dynamic results select a well defined straight stripe. Think for a moment which way the squares have to be folded initially, and play with the material before you actually stitch anything in place. Balance the stripes carefully: having a stripe in the centre of the folded triangle may give the most effective result.

"Tucked In" Squares have lots of potential.
Will you ever sleep tonight?

Inserted "Tucked In" Squares

What would happen if a "Tucked In" square was inserted into a seam? I tried and discovered that a **bias** cut square had the greatest twiddlable possibilities.

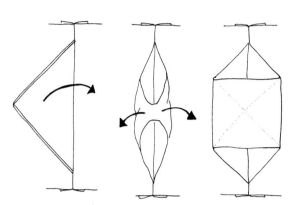

Make up one bias cut square into the "Tucked In" shape (pages 19 - 20: Stages 1 - 2). After folding, baste the raw edges. Sandwich the shape between two strips of material, sew the seam. Remove basting, open back seam, press flat. Turn to the R/S, lift the inserted section, pull the sides apart and squash down carefully. Be gentle - don't flatten the life out of it. The creases from the original pressing should appear in the centre. Now, what can you do with it?

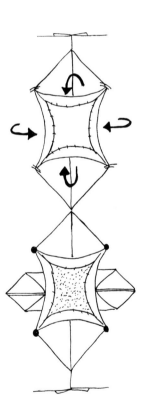

All the edges of this newly formed central square roll - they are on the bias! (If the square is <u>not</u> bias cut to begin with, then these edges will roll much less.) Secure the four corners of the central square with a small stitch and roll the sides. Consider laying a contrasting coloured piece of fabric first, then rolling the edges (as per Cathedral Windows). Tuck smaller folded squares underneath the central shape on either side.

To make an interesting corner piece for a quilt or hanging - set a "Tucked In" shape diagonally in a square. Have a row of them for a border, on a garment or down a bag.

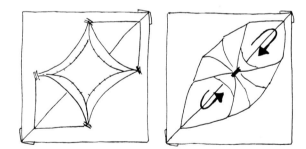

For a different textural design, bring opposite sides of the central shape together as shown in right-hand diagram above, secure with a stitch and add a bead or two. The shape can be as large as you like, made from any fabric, inserted anywhere you fancy, then twiddled, fiddled and manoeuvred. You could even combine eight in a block design...........

Inserted "Tucked In" Squares
Block

Finished size 36cm (**14$\frac{1}{4}$"**) exc. S/A
Seam allowance 0.65cm ($\frac{1}{4}$")
Apologies to those working in metric, there are some odd measurements.

Cut: Four 20cm (**8"**) squares
from background material

Eight 12cm (**4$\frac{3}{4}$"**) squares*
for the textured sections
*Squares can be cut with all sides on bias or straight grain - your choice (see page 23)

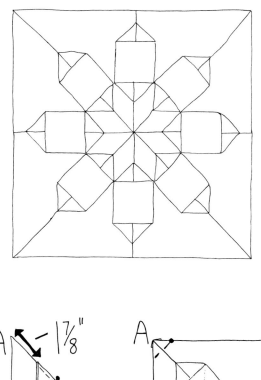

1. Cut all four 20cm (**8"**) squares in half on the diagonal forming eight triangles. Fold all eight 12cm (**4$\frac{3}{4}$"**) squares into "Tucked In" shapes (pages 19 - 20: Stages 1 - 2). Ensure both sets of folds (either side of triangle) are flush, adjust if necessary; baste the raw edges to retain the shape.

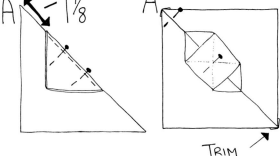

Take one of these shapes and one of the eight background triangles. Place the "Tucked In" shape on R/S of background triangle **exactly 4.5cm (1$\frac{7}{8}$")** from the tip (**A**); align all raw edges. Lay another triangle on top sandwiching the shape; sew the bias edge using 0.65 cm ($\frac{1}{4}$") S/A - try not to stretch the seam. Open the square out, remove basting and press back seam open and flat; trim 'ears' or points from square. Make three more squares using the remaining six background triangles and three more "Tucked In" shapes. To prevent errors in construction, mark the **A** corner on all four pieces with a pin or make a light pencil dot. (The **A** corners meet at the centre.) Carefully flatten the inserts, pin in place - do not press yet.

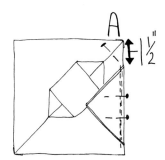

2. Take one stitched square, place one "Tucked In" shape **exactly 3.8cm (1$\frac{1}{2}$")** from **A**; line up all raw edges, pin in place and baste.

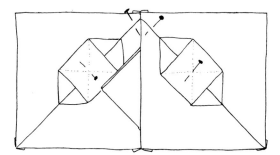

Take another stitched square and join both together matching seams. Press seam open and flat.

Repeat with the remaining two stitched squares and one more "Tucked In" shape. Both halves of the block are now completed, and there are two shapes left.

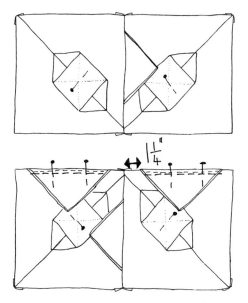

3. Take one half of the block; lay the last two **exactly 3.2cm (1¼")** from the centre seam, pin in place and baste. Remove pins by **A** before stitching the two halves together. Match all seams and points in the centre.

4. Flatten all remaining "Tucked In" shapes, with a little jiggle they should all touch in a ring. Press carefully. If the pieces don't quite touch, does it matter? Beads can be added to conceal the junctions and if all the seams don't quite match up in the centre - come on - embellish with a button ☺.

Now play: roll edges; tuck bits in; bring the sides of the central shape together (photograph opposite page 43); lay another fabric in the centre and roll the sides over. There are many twiddleable possibilities, have a play (more ideas on page 23). Remember - nothing is wrong - it is just a little different!

"Baby in a Basket"

Finally, use a "Tucked In" square as a textural insert. Take a square of any size, make up as instructed (pages 19 - 20: Stages 1 - 2).

Fold the top two folds (top one from either side) to lie flush either side of the centre as in diagram 2. This could be used for a textural edging.

For a more manipulated effect, fold outside sections inwards, overlapping them evenly at the centre of the shape. Baste layers and trim excess material from the base. Voilà - a "Baby in a Basket"!

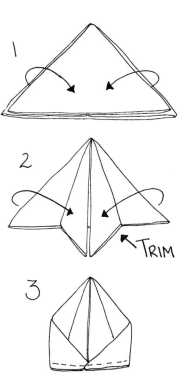

Why the name? Ask Ada! This natty little idea came to me whilst I was teaching at Missenden Abbey. As usual, the perennial problem of a name, so Ada (one of my students) said "Its just like a baby in a basket!" So there you are.

Missenden Abbey is a rather superb place, terribly upright, where they hold Adult Education weekend courses and summer schools, with lots of excellent tuition and the grub is none too bad either. You can stay in the Abbey or in the locality. I have always felt that if one has B & B at Missenden, it most certainly does not stand for Booze and Bonking but very much for Bed and Breakfast!

I disgraced myself there on one occasion. It was the Tutors' Supper and I was sat sitting opposite a fairly severe looking gentleman who turned and solemnly enquired what I taught. Unfortunately, the large glass of sherry beforehand had lowered my inhibitions, and I flippantly responded with "Sex and Stitching!" Being of a polite nature and appreciating that I should return his question, I asked what he did "Buddhism and Philosophy" was his somewhat sparse reply. End of conversation. I know very little about either subject and it was fairly clear from his face that 'sex and stitching' did not do a lot for him either. I retired after the main course.

Insert a "Baby in a Basket" in any seam for textural decoration. Pop one in a pocket, stuff one into a 'Trumpet' (technique from **'Tucks Textures & Pleats'**).

Use them on garments, quilts, hangings etc. Why not have an edging made of "Babies in Baskets" rather than Prairie Points. Why not use one as a tab with the tip anchored down with a button? For more textural definition roll the folded edges back and see what happens.

One last suggestion.... why not make these "Tucked In" squares in two colours with the central section different from the outside? Try it and see.

Make the square out of two differently coloured rectangles, fold it and see what happens. Just think about a little about how you fold it - one way works and the other one doesn't. Have fun!

"Tucked In" Squares with "Baby in a Basket" border

"Tucked In" Hexagons

If you can "tuck in" a square why not a hexagon? Once more, lots of possibilities for textural innovation and manipulative play.

As previously mentioned, crisp and firmly woven medium-weight materials are very suitable for this design. Spray starch any thin, floppy or well-washed fabrics to restore a bit of the 'body'. Starching should be done before cutting, as squirting small pieces of material with generous amounts of starch, then vigorously ironing, may result in distorted shapes.

1. Cut four identical hexagons of any size and the same colour. Use one of the hexagonal templates on page 109 or make your own (instructions on page 67).

Cutting out hexagons can be time consuming. Save fabric by drawing round the template the required number of times; the shape tessellates (fits together); consequently less fabric is wasted between the shapes. Cut out the pieces carefully.

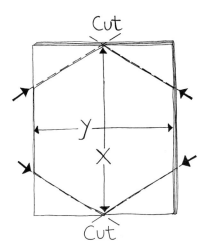

Speed up the process by cutting a strip of material **x**cm **(x")** wide; *x is the widest measurement (point to point) of the selected hexagon.* Cut this strip into *y*cm *(y")* lengths; *y is the distance between any two opposite parallel sides of the selected hexagon.* Cut one section **x**cm/" x **y**cm/" for each hexagon required. Pile the sections carefully on top of each other (R/S or W/S up - doesn't matter). Place template on top and cut off all four corners.

At least ten or even twelve hexagons can be cut at the same time if you are using a rotary cutter. Carefully layer all the sections matching raw edges, push firmly on the cutter - give it a bit of welly! This method wastes a certain amount of material but is much faster.

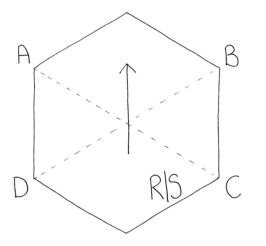

Look carefully at the grain line of the material and find the two straight grain sides (opposite each other). Press one hexagon in half (R/S out) on **A/C** diagonal; open out and refold shape on **B/D** diagonal (R/S out), press. Try not to obliterate the first diagonal crease as you press the second diagonal one. Both pressed creases form an **X** shape with top and bottom of **X** at the sides (on straight grain). Press two more hexagons in the same way - leave one hexagon un-ironed. Both creases on each hexagon must be on the R/S of the fabric.

2. Fold one of the pressed hexagons in half (R/S out). Slightly lift the top layer of the folded hexagon and tuck **E** inside. **E** folds easily inside because the fabric bends neatly on the pressed creases. Repeat with **F** on the other side to form a diamond shape. There are two folds on the adjacent sides of the diamond - **A/D** and **B/C**, align the edges of each set of folds accurately and press carefully. (**D** and **C** are on top with **A** and **B** folds beneath.)

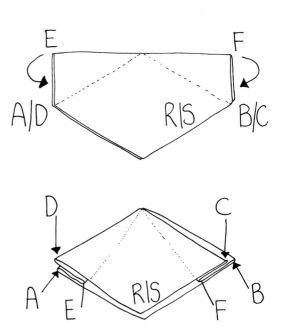

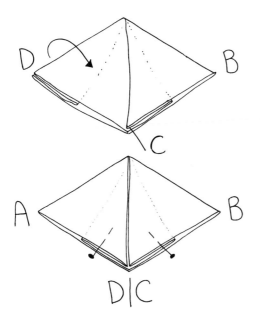

3. Carefully lift **C** and **D** folds only (**A** and **B** remain in place); bring **C** and **D** to the centre of the pressed diamond, pin in place. Press shape lightly. Repeat the method with the other two pressed hexagons to make three identically folded diamonds.

4. Fit the three pressed and folded diamonds on to the last (unpressed) hexagon matching all the edges, pin all folds carefully. At **G**, sew the tips of all the three diamonds to the hexagon beneath with a few small stitches. Baste round the outside, keeping stitching close to the raw edges and using longest machine stitch.

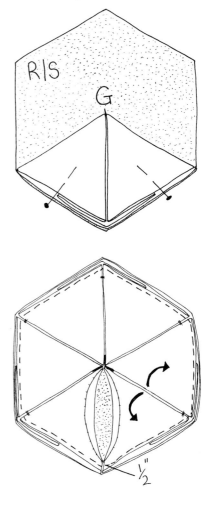

5. Measure 1cm (**$^1/_2$"**) along the folds (from each point of hexagon) and stitch the layers together; roll back both folds to make a petal shape and slip stitch in place. Stitch the entire length of the rolled back edge or just secure it in the centre. (The base hexagon is revealed in every other section.)

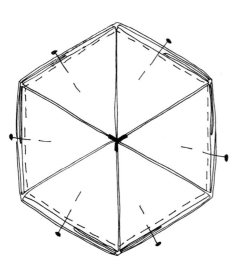

All the rolled folds can be stitched down by machine using the Blind Hem stitch (page 8); using thread to match material. Other machine stitches could be used for extra ornamentation.

Design Development

The possibilities are endless, for example try altering the size of the petal shapes by anchoring every alternate set of folds **more** than 1cm (**$^1/_2$"**) from raw edges to give three large petal shapes and three smaller ones.

Does the base hexagon have to be the same colour as the others? How about a different one? Why not have different shades in each oval hole - make the base hexagon out of two or three separate colours (seam two or three pieces together - hide seams underneath the folded diamonds). Join several shapes together and make a design feature from the different colours.

Experiment with sheer or transparent materials and hang against the light. Be very decadent and use velvet as the base hexagon with lurex/lamé for the top ones. Lay other pieces of material underneath the folds before you roll anything back - try different colours. Add a few folded squares in relevant places.

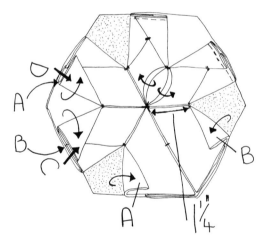

What about playing with the pieces - why not twiddle the folds a little before basting round the edge? Cut four 15cm (**6"**) hexagons and make them up to Stage 4 (page 28). Measure 3cm (**$1^1/_4$"**) from the centre down the folds, and anchor all layers together with a small stitch. (This measurement can be changed). Select one of the diamonds, lift **A** and **B** flaps and fold in - towards the centre of the diamond; keep all raw edges together on outside edge. These folded edges will pull - panic not!

Open out **C** and **D**; pull back to overlap **B** and **A**. Pin carefully. Secure the overlapped folds with a small stitch through all the layers. Baste round the raw edges before rolling any or all folded edges. Secure rolled folds with hand or machine stitching.

Just think of the design possibilities if several of these are joined together!

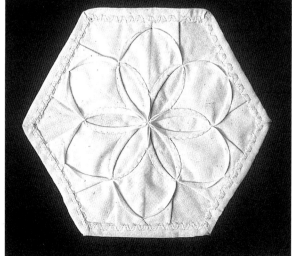

"Tucked In" Triangles

You'll never believe this, but the same sort of "tucking in" principle can be applied to triangles. Yet again, any number of innovative designs can be created with a bit of jiggling, juggling, twiddling and tweaking.

As shown in the last two sections, there is very little sewing, most of the design is created by folding and manipulating. (For fabric advice see page 19.)

Those of you who believe in starting in the middle of a chapter and guessing the first part - read or work through the other methods before launching into this section.

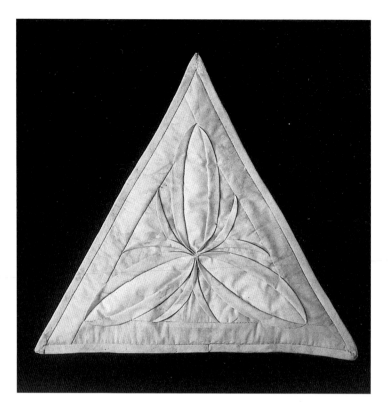

For a successfully manipulated result, be careful with the initial folding - keep the bias and straight grain in the designated places.

Each triangular segment requires four triangles - three for the top and one for the base triangle. These can all be the same colour or you can have any combination that you choose. *Experiment with the same coloured shapes first, then alter the colours later.*

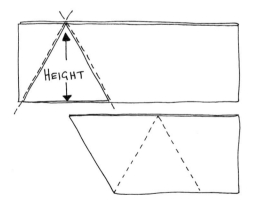

Use the 60° template given on page 108 or construct your own. Draw round template and cut out. The fastest way to cut triangles is to measure the height of the triangle; cut strip of the fabric this measurement (cut strips across the material - selvedge to selvedge). **Fold the strip in half widthways**, place template on top and cut (cutting two at a time). By flipping the fabric over or by turning the template, you can rapidly cut the necessary number of triangles.

If you have not got a rotary cutter; cut the strip, fold it in half, lay template on top and draw in either side. Pin fabric layers together, then cut on the drawn lines.

1. To make **one** unit, cut **four** fabric triangles. Take one of the triangles and fold it in half R/S out, press; refold on another side and repeat; finally fold last side in half and press again. All three creases should be apparent and will cross in the centre of the triangle. Try not to completely obliterate the first and second creases as you press: take care and iron with a little TLC (tender loving care - not a strange type of iron), don't flatten the material into total abject submission.

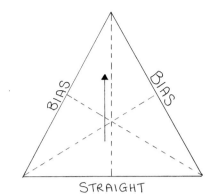

STRAIGHT

2. ***Watch the straight grain line***. Lay the triangle **W/S up** on a flat surface, straight grain running top to bottom. If you can't see the straight grain, gently pull the sides of the shape, two sides will stretch (bias grain) and one will not (straight grain). Fold triangle in half bringing **A** to **C**; R/S of fabric is now uppermost, and you will have a fold from **B** to the new point **D**. (It may help to label the points, mark lightly using a pencil.)

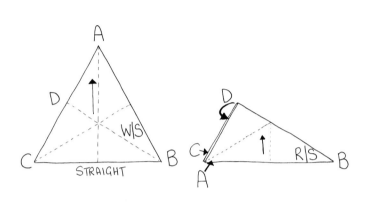

Lift **A** point up and tuck in **D** (goes inside the folded triangle). There are now two folds (**A** and **C**) together at one end of the triangle and only one fold at **B** (other end). Press very lightly.

3. Lift fold at **A**, open out sides and flatten down in the centre of the triangle (forms a diamond shape - half the diamond hangs outside the triangle). The two folds of material inside (underneath) the diamond should butt together - tweak into place if necessary. Pin the layers, and resist the temptation to trim any excess fabric.

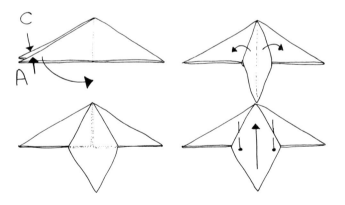

Peer closely at the diamond shape and you will be able to see the straight grain of the material running up the centre, consequently all the sides of the diamond shaped section will be on the bias and will .... guess what? Roll!! "By Jingo it's clever", she says!

Repeat the entire exercise with the remaining two top triangles making three identically folded sections with all straight grains in the same place. One un-ironed and unfolded triangle remains for the base of the design.

4. Lay all three pressed shapes on to the base triangle, aligning longest edge of each folded shape with an outside edge of the base triangle. Butt up the folds carefully. Pin well. Secure the tips of all three shapes to the base triangle with a few small stitches. These will show - don't just hack it together. If your hand sewing is poor or the points don't quite fit, then buttons work a treat!

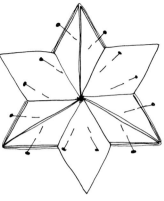

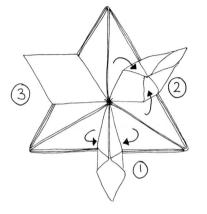

5. Now - it is make your mind up time! The central diamond-shaped sections can be manipulated in several ways; it is advisable to manipulate them before basting round the outside edges of the triangle. Why not: **1)** bring the outer folds of the central diamond section to meet in the centre of each long side; **2)** fold the sides of the diamond section inwards and overlap them, or **3)** just leave the shape as it is?

Whichever option you choose, pin in place, trim any excess fabric then baste round the outer raw edges. All the various folded edges of all the shapes can be rolled back for a little textural creativity. The base fabric will be revealed in the three larger rolled-back sections (diagram below).

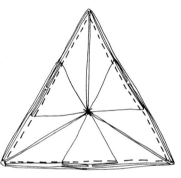

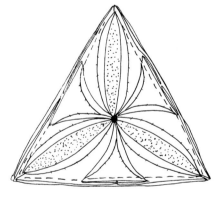

Now think of the possibilities. Join six units to make a hexagon with a different coloured base material. Watch the straight grain - be consistent.

Link the units and add extra colour or a different texture in the diamond spaces - lay a smaller piece of fabric inside this space, the raw edges of fabric being covered by rolling the edges of the diamond shape. Embellish the petal spaces with embroidery.

What else can you do?

How about inserting the shape into a seam? I did wonder if it was worth the effort and having had a little experiment - yes, it is.

Press the triangle as in Stage 1 page 31, making the three creases. ***Watch the straight grain line*** - this triangle has the straight grain running in a different direction from the last ones. Lay out the shape with **straight grain on the left-hand side** and fold the **A/C** side. Lift **A** and tuck **D** in. (Folding the triangle in this manner ensures that the external edges will roll.) Align the two folds at **A/C** end, pin layers and baste the raw edges. Keep basting within the seam allowance.

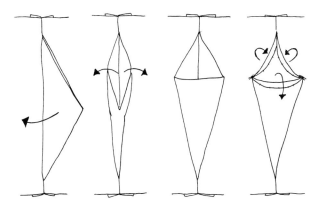

Sandwich the shape between two other pieces of material and play! Lift, pull apart and flatten. (This final shape is similar to the 'Trumpet' from '**Tucks Textures & Pleats**' but a little more elongated and possibly a trifle more elegant.)

Secure the corners with a few small stitches and roll the edges. Very small folded squares can be inserted into the pocket first if you wish. Explore the potential and see what happens.

The "Tucked In" triangle can be inserted into any seam. Put them in a row and use as a panel for a wearable: do they all have to be the same size? And why not have one up, one down - alternate the direction? Stitch six between the seams of six 60° (equilateral) triangles or try an Eight-pointed Star as in the picture below (if the centre points do not quite match then you know the answer .....A button! Use them in a border design or anywhere else you fancy!

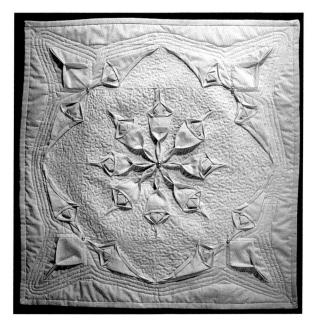

Tuck and Scrunch

Travelling with bags full of quilts and sewing materials means very little room for personal things like clothing. Laundry becomes a perennial problem, not so much the washing but the drying of clothes. Hotels do have laundry services but the price is astronomical and the timing does not always fit one's schedule. No good them returning your personal things when you have flown on to the next place as it would mean knickers in the post all over the world.

Washing the bits out in the bath is fine, the shower a little more difficult and hand basins for anything large is a nightmare especially when the plug will not retain the water. Once washed though the fun begins......

Roll up items in a towel and jump on the towel to get excess moisture out and to perform your daily exercise. Suspend from any surface. Lampshades are excellent as the heat from the bulb helps with the drying. Unhappily hotels have the put the kibosh on this by replacing ordinary bulbs with neon ones that give off no heat whatsoever. Hair dryers are quite useful and a sock fits nicely on the end.

Another idea is to use the ceiling fan: thought of this in Florida, noted the speed settings, arranged everything on the blades and turned on slow speed. Collected all the bits and pieces from the four corners of the room.

But the best solution is the microwave. Many motels in New Zealand have microwaves in a sort of kitchenette arrangement. Did you know that five minutes on high dries three pairs of knickers and a bra brilliantly? Just be careful, don't put under-wired items in because they tend to spark a bit and this damages the fibres. Little hooks and eyes are no problem. The great thing about this - all the lingerie comes out all warm and cosy!

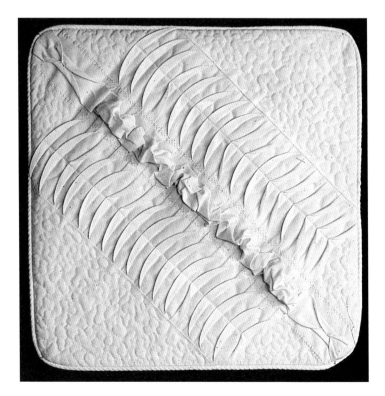

Photograph: Bias cut Tuck and Scrunch (page 38).

Tuck and Scrunch

Take a strip of fabric of any length or width and combine two essentially simple, textural, twiddling and fiddling techniques for a fancy panel or insert. This technique is great for garments, bags and cushions, and would make an intriguingly unusual quilt border.

Chintzes and other crisply finished materials are easy to work with as they crease well but try it with all kinds of fabric. Most of the examples shown in the photographs are made from medium-weight firmly woven calico.

In my opinion Tuck and Scrunch is best constructed on the machine as it takes a month of Sundays by hand. If you can sew a straightish line then why not give it a whirl? Try the method first, then create your own 'Tuck and Scrunch' design - change the spacing and size of the centre section as well as the depth of the tucks. Explore the creative possibilities of flexing the tucks in different ways. There is a bit of preparation before you leap into the fray.

For a **finished** band approximately 15cm (**6"**) x 52cm (**20"**), cut a strip of material 23cm (**9"**) wide x full width of fabric i.e. 115cm (**45"**). Cut the strip across the material (from selvedge to selvedge). Fold strip (R/S out) in half along the length, pin layers together and press gently. Rule a line 3cm (**1^1/$_4$"**) away from fold, the full length of the material. The ruled line won't show, but draw faintly using a hard sharp pencil not an ink pen or Biro (sometimes these bleed in the wash).

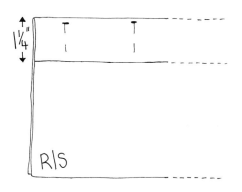

1. Match thread colour to fabric on both the top spool and bottom bobbin. Sew along the pencil line (regular/normal stitch i.e. 2^1/$_2$ - 3). This makes a large fat tuck or pleat. Open and flatten/squash the tuck over the seam underneath, positioning the flattened tuck evenly and equally over the seam. The pressed crease should be in the centre.

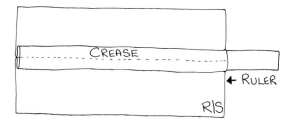

Push a thin slat/ruler/piece of stiff card approximately 2.5cm (1") wide down the inside of the tuck. Wiggle the tuck so that it is equally spaced over the seam, and press.

2. On the **R/S**, make small marks at 4cm (**1^1/$_2$"**) intervals down the **outside edge of both long sides and on either side of the central pressed tuck**. Mark lightly using a hard sharp pencil. To reduce inaccuracies and save awkward mathematics, make a card template 4cm (**1^1/$_2$"**) wide by approximately 20cm (**8"**) long and use this as a measuring

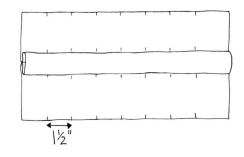

3. Fold the fabric on the first set of marks; the pencil mark lies exactly on the **edge of the fabric fold**. If you wish, pin the fold in place. Measuring from fold, sew a 1cm ($^3/_8$") seam (normal stitch length) across the material towards the central tuck - use measurements marked on throat plate as a guide. Alternatively move the needle position, setting the needle 1cm ($^3/_8$") from edge of presser foot (see page 8 Seam Allowances). Align edge of presser foot with the fabric fold.

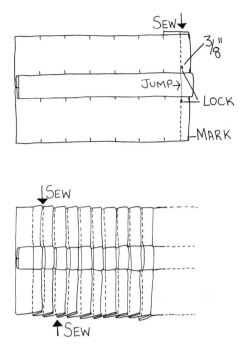

Stop stitching approximately 0.65cm ($^1/_4$") from the flattened centre tuck; lock threads - reduce stitch length to minimum, use the machine's 'stitch tie-off' button or drop the feed dogs and sew on the spot.

Jump over centre tucked section (cut threads later), leave a 0.65cm ($^1/_4$") gap before commencing stitching on the other side; lock threads at start of seam and sew to the end of the fold. This makes the first tuck. Turn the work round (go in the opposite direction), fold on the next (second) set of marks and sew the next tuck. Repeat on the third set of marks etc. One 1cm ($^3/_8$") tuck is made on every set of pencil marks. Continue in this manner until you reach the end of the strip.

It is important to sew up and down the material; working from one side to the other; failing to do so can result in a distorted strip. Keep the bulk of the fabric on the left-hand side of machine as usual. As you sew back and forth across the material you will discover that the tucks will be underneath on every other row of stitching - this is normal - don't panic, it happens to everyone! Save thread - sew on to a thread saver (see page 6).

4. Continue sewing the tucks until the piece is the right length for your chosen project. Carefully press all the tucks in the same direction on R/S, turn to W/S and press again. Don't worry if the seams of tucks look a little uneven - all will be well when you twiddle and many an anomaly will be hidden in the texture!

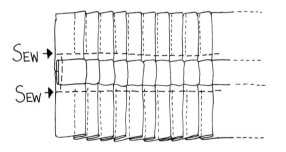

5. Cut all the 'jumped over' threads on *both* sides of the centre section, press again if necessary. Turn the work so that the folded edges of the tucks are facing you. Down either side of the central tuck: sew approximately 0.65 ($^1/_4$") from the folded edge - rule a faint line or run the side of the presser foot along the fold with the machine needle set 0.65 ($^1/_4$") away from presser foot edge.

Why not use a decorative stitch for a little extra embellishment? This adds interest and covers any overgenerous pencil marks lying alongside the central tuck.

6. Now - a little magic! Carefully pull the centre tuck out from the tucked folds. It comes out scrunched up - 'lumpy-bumpy' for want of a better description. Tweak and twitch the folds gently to achieve a pleasingly ruched effect. (Any section that 'catches' may have one of the 'jumped' threads still uncut.) If you pull too hard and the scrunchy texture is lost, carefully replace the tuck in the original folds and try again. To retain the scrunchiness, catch the fabric down (through all layers) in relevant places and/or decorate with some beads/buttons. Baste close to the raw edges to hold the tucks in place - use the longest stitch length.

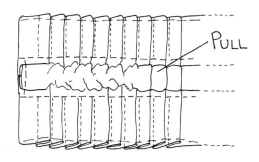

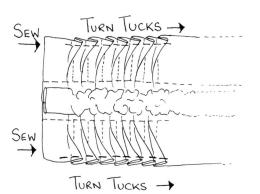

Think for a moment .... before you baste, why not try a little extra textural manipulation? Twist the tucks in the reverse direction - i.e. flip 'em over. Sew down both sides of the piece and as you go, turn the tucks. Keep the stitching within the 0.65cm ($^{1}/_{4}$") S/A. It is easier to do if you start sewing with the tucks facing away and flip (pull) them back towards you, but the choice is yours.

To make a cushion/pillow or one side of a bag; trim the Tuck and Scrunch strip to the desired dimension; if necessary make a border by adding strips to the relevant sides. Place the correctly sized section on to some wadding/batting and pin in place. Embellish the border with a few lines of decorative stitch. Finally baste the outside edges to hold the layers together (use the longest stitch length or a wide zigzag).

Playtime

Now you understand the technique - so what else can be done with it? Why not make an attractive cushion/pillow with a diagonally centred Tuck and Scrunch band (see photograph on page 39)?

Cut one end of your straight strip into a right-angle, and start the markings 1cm ($^{1}/_{2}$") from the angled cut. Make the tucks as described in Stages 3 - 4 but leave enough space at the end of the strip to cut another right-angle. Follow the rest of the method in Stages 5 - 6.

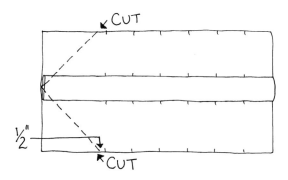

Square off the design by adding a right-angled triangle either side of the completed Tuck and Scrunch band. Increase the size with a border.

Why not turn the tucks in different directions as shown in the photograph? It makes a delightfully pretty panel for a garment. Construct the design by making an even number of tucks i.e. pairs of tucks. Press all the tucks in the same direction. As you sew down the centre section twist one of each pair towards the other one so that they touch or overlap. Repeat with the next pair etc. On the outer edges reverse the procedure so that each tuck twists in the opposite direction. It's ingenious!

To some people this seems easy to understand, but others can puzzle over the description. Here is an alternative explanation.

Make an even number of tucks (i.e. divisible by two). You will now have pairs of tucks or let's call them couples of tucks. A very common couple that we all understand is Mummy and Daddy, divide the tucks into sets of Mummies and Daddies. As you sew down the centre of the panel, twist each Mummy so that she 'kisses' each Daddy (marital harmony). You may well find that Mummy actually puts her arms around Daddy (tucks overlap), makes for real lovey-doveyiness! BUT when it comes to sewing the outer edges, our happy couples have an enormous row and turn away from each other. As you sew down the edge you will find that Mummy kisses the Daddy from next door!!! Oh dear - another common situation! Will divorce threaten?

Explaining the tuck-twisting manoeuvre in this fashion isn't doing my reputation any good at all but if it makes for clarity of understanding then I don't mind. Not everybody teaches sex and stitching!

Add some lace, ribbon or braid to decorate or conceal any irregularities in the stitch. Attach to the work with a straight or a zigzag stitch, laying the appliqué over the previous sewing. Use matching thread to the appliqué.

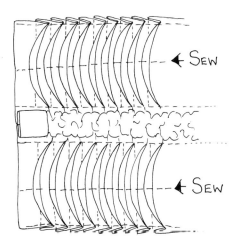

What about cutting the initial strip on the bias and much wider? Follow the same procedure as before. As the strip is wider, the tucks will be much longer. Press all the tucks as described in Stage 4. Sew down either side of the centre section with all the tucks facing the same direction and repeat on the outside edges. (All tucks are firmly anchored on both ends.) Rule a light pencil line down the middle of each tucked section and sew (following the line), reversing the direction of the tucks as you go. The tucks will roll back in arcs because the fabric was cut on the bias to begin with (see photograph on page 34). Truly splendiferous!

For a softer effect with less stitching, why not hand pleat the fabric omitting the sewing of each individual tuck?

Mark the spacings as before then fold the fabric on the marks, pinning the tucks individually, or speed up the process by omitting the pinning and just fold the fabric on the marks as you stitch down either side of the central section. Take a little care as the folds can easily become uneven and the outer edges may distort.

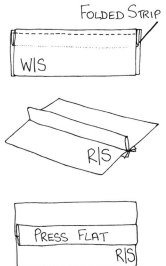

Change the colour of the central scrunched section by joining two separate strips (for the horizontal tucks) with another different coloured fabric inserted in the seam. Cut the correct sized pieces (*remember to add S/As where needed*), fold centre strip in half, R/S outside, and sandwich between the other two strips. Press seams open and flat.

The central striped section in the navy and white bag (colour photographs opposite page 18) was constructed by cutting two equal strips (cut on the horizontal - across the stripes) and inserting a piece of the striped material (cut vertically - down one stripe).

Try the technique in various materials; change the tuck size, direction of twist or dimensions of the centre panel. Double up on the design and have two rows of Scrunch with tucks in between. It makes a very pretty inserted frilly panel for a dress or any other garment. If the strip needs to be longer than the full width of the material, join lengths together first using a small seam, press seam open and flat. Endeavour to hide the seamed junction underneath a tuck, jiggle the marked spacings until this can be achieved.

Have a play and see what else can be done with a little bit of 'Tuck and Scrunch'!

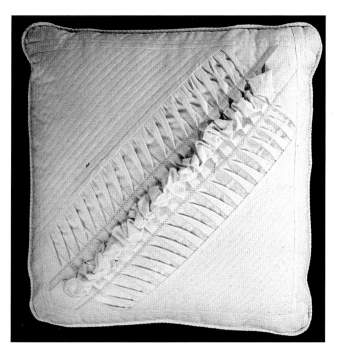

Stick and Scrunch

The inspiration for this came from Georgio Armani's wonderful collection of clothing in the Guggenheim Museum in New York. The man and I flew in for three days sightseeing in December! We froze on the ferry, gawped at the lights, walked miles and miles, up and down the Empire State, ate in delis and posh places, spluttered at the prices, wondered at the amazingness of that incredible city and went to the museums.

We did the MOMA, the Met, the this and the that, saved the Guggenheim until last, as a **real treat for himself**. Ah, the paintings we would see displayed on those carefully angled walls, the ambience etc. etc. We arrived, his turn to pay - $12 each entrance fee. First exhibit was a dress from Georgio Armani, marvellous. I lingered. Second exhibit was another dress by the same guy. Oh superb! I lingered longer; he moved on up the spiral to look at the paintings. Ten minutes later, I was staring at the fourth exhibit - more dresses by Armani when he came rushing towards me. "I've been robbed", he cried. "Of what?" I replied somewhat panic stricken, visualising no money, no credit cards and being marooned in New York. "Of $24!" he said.

The entire museum was devoted to Armani, twenty years of his designs, not a painting in sight - all stored away. Poor guy, thwarted and considerably miffed, he retired to wait while I had a lovely time pottering round the garments getting some smashing ideas.

This is very quick and easy, great for embellishing, a real wow for embroiderers. You need some fusible glue web (such as Bondaweb/Wundaweb/Heat 'n Bond) and two squares of fabric (for alternative method see next page).

Cut one larger 25cm **(10")** square and one smaller 20cm **(8")** square of material. Use a long stitch (hand or machine) and gather the outer edges of the larger square, pulling the threads until the sides fit the smaller 20cm **(8")** one.

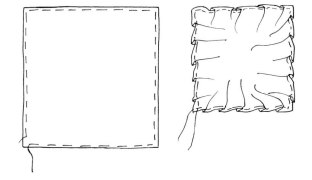

Adhere the fusible glue web to the 20cm **(8")** square and peel off the protective paper.

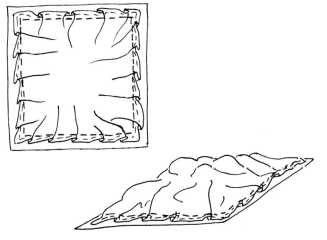

Lay the gathered section onto the **sticky** side of the second square, ease the sides to fit. Pin the layers together and baste round the raw edges.

Arrange the excess material evenly over the smaller square and pin down in random places. When the top layer is arranged to your satisfaction, press the surface very carefully. Use point of the iron to press the fabrics together in specific areas. The heat of the iron will create adhesion between the top fabric and the under layer. Avoid pressing the pins - the heads may melt.

Any unattached areas can be secured with beads or embroidery (hand or machine).

Alternative Method:
Replace the fusible web and smaller square of fabric with a square of iron-on stabiliser (Vilene in UK or Pellon in USA). Gather the larger square to fit edges of stabiliser, baste together and press as described above.

Design Ideas

Use striped material for a really zany effect. Experiment with transparent materials (check for heat resistance first). Embellish with machine or hand stitching adding beads, sequins or buttons as you go. Why not fabric paint some of the areas or spray a dye on top; fix dye or paint as in manufacturers' instructions?

Does the panel have to be square? No. Any shape will work - use up old scraps of material. For a more generous scrunched effect use a much larger top section. (This may not stick down so readily and a few little stitches may be required in pertinent places.)

Uses for the Idea

This is just a tactile textural notion that could be inserted into a garment, used for the centre of a design, included in a landscape or used for the lid of a box. Why not make several panels of the technique, embellish each one with different stitches, bead and sequins then stitch together for a distinctly different hanging?

Photograph: "Stick and Scrunch" panels embellished in different threads with a variety of stitch patterns, beads and buttons. (Cynthia Groves)

Textured Piecing

I threatened tales of steamy travel in the foreword... Had the steamy part with kettle cooking and laundering, now it's travel - car travel to be specific. Since I started globetrotting I have had to drive in other countries; not all countries drive on the same side. Of course, I have always believed that in Britain we drive on the right (correct) side of the road, although it actually is the left, which is highly confusing to begin with especially if you can't tell your right from your left.

Driving in America for the first time was discombobulating to put it mildly. First, I had to hire a car. Could I understand what the young lady said? Subtle difference in language! With grave difficulty, we sorted out price, time and insurance but when she enquired what model I wanted .....failure! "Wanna a Toyotacamrysedanblur or a Chevvysomthingorotherelse" she said. I looked blank, she repeated, blank again. Exasperated she said "Do yer wanna green one or a blue one?" I had the green one!

Into the car park to find the car, actually it is a parking lot (totally correct as there are lots of cars parked!). Slightly rattled by the booking fiasco, I opened the car door and got in. No steering wheel! Whoops - it is America - try the other side. Hoping no one had noticed, I went to the right side, in fact it is the left side - even more confusion, and got in. Okey-dokey, start engine, put in gear and it won't move, nothing happens. It is an automatic (I only drive ones with gears - stick shifts), surely all you do is start the engine and it does all the rest for you? No. I pressed everything, opened the boot/bonnet (trunk/hood) several times, adjusted my seat up and down and eventually by a sheer fluke, must have hit the brake. Magic! We were off.

Out on to the highway and it is fantastic, wide roads, not much traffic. Wound the car up a bit to 90 mph then remembered the speed limits - better behave - it's not England. Turn the music on - Country and Western (not quite me but when in Rome ...). What else can one do? Try cruise control - amazing! You can take both feet off the pedals, probably can paint your toenails as you drive. Then a McDonalds loomed up - coffee time? Crikey, it is a drive thru! Collect coffee, put it in the cup holder and swig it as you go. I felt really American. Smashing!

Hours later, on a country road, there were flashing red lights by a railway crossing. The road was deserted but I stopped, and waited for the train. And waited and waited, nothing happened, it's probably a very big train, an enormous train - possibly the biggest train in the entire USA. Ten minutes later, another car came towards me, slowed down and crossed the track. Nobody told me that the red flashing lights were a warning of the railway crossing and not an indication of the train coming. What a lulu! I would probably be still sat sitting there today if that other car had not come along.

It takes time to get acclimatised to the driving. There are differences - turning right against a red light, undertaking other cars, road junctions are numbered x miles from some predetermined place and not in sequence (264 is followed by 291). All most confusing. No one tells you that the Sam Houston TLWY is not a Travelway but a Tollway and the lady (?) at the booth got somewhat annoyed by my huge dollar bill. I didn't know there were that many expletives. The traffic in my line was held up for ages!

Razzle - Dazzle (48"
square): Textured Piecing
with Petal Pattern border.
Machine pieced and
quilted. (Jennie Rayment)

Holey Stars Tablecloth:
created from medium
weight calico/muslin.
Machine pieced.
(Jennie Rayment)

Rug 83 (38" diameter): features "Tucked in" Squares and Triangles, Twisted Origami Hexagon (5 Pleats), Truly Tucked-up Band, with "Baby in a Basket" border. Pieced from forty 9º sections. Machine pieced and quilted. (Jennie Rayment)

Left - 'Seamless' Scalloped Cross cushion (16" square). Right - Lampshade with Truly Tucked-up Band, bunch of Floral Fantasies and Holey Star mat. All items machine pieced and quilted.

(Jennie Rayment)

Textured Piecing

What on earth is Textured Piecing? The title describes it well - the design is pieced (as in sewing the bits together) with a textural element created by the construction. There are edges to roll and little pockets to stuff and places to insert more little folded thingies. This idea was to be called "Curvy Seams for Stressed out Quilters" but I think Textured Piecing is a little more succinct.

Use the Textured Piecing technique to revitalise and revamp many of your favourite patchwork blocks by creating a new curvaceous look, or add a distinctly different nuance to border designs - it's just absolutely brain bogglingly fascinating. There aren't any complicated bits to cut out or seams to sew. As all the pieces are either squares and/or rectangles life is a bowl of cherries. Personally, I think this is a bit of a misnomer; cherries are tasty, sweet, juicy and definitely delectable until you get to the pip! No pip here though, everything is sweet and easy throughout, just try it and see.

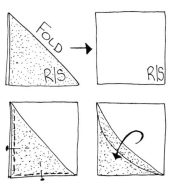

The simplest form of Textured Piecing requires two equal-sized and maybe differently coloured squares. Fold one square in half diagonally (on bias and R/S out) and put it on top of the other square (R/S up), aligning all the raw edges. Pin the layers together, and baste round raw edges. This creates a square apparently 'split' into two equal triangles (sometimes called a divided or half-divided square). BUT... the folded bias edge of the applied (top) square will roll back to form an arc. In addition, the little pocket can be stuffed (padded) with a folded square of some sort inserted.

Just think of the difference you can make to a whole range of patchwork designs! The basic Amish Friendship Star (pictured below), an ordinary Eight Pointed star or many other similar patterns would look radically different if the relevant parts of the design are replaced with these units - au revoir straight edges - hello curves. As a bonus, this technique is much easier to construct with no triangular templates needed, just rotary-cut squares.

Amish Friendship Star

Finished size 30cm **(12")** exc. S/As
Seam Allowance 0.75cm (**$^1/_4$"**)

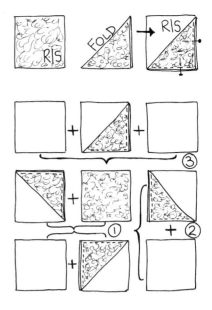

Cut: Five 12cm (**$4^1/_2$"**) squares - *Star* (patterned parts)
     Eight 12cm (**$4^1/_2$"**) squares - *Background*

1. Press one 12cm (**$4^1/_2$"**) *Star* square in half diagonally to form a triangular piece (R/S out). Pin to one 12cm (**$4^1/_2$"**) *background* square aligning all raw edges; baste round edge and remove pins. Repeat with other three *Star* pieces and three more *background* squares to make four units in total. Take the last 12cm (**$4^1/_2$"**) *Star* square and the last four 12cm (**$4^1/_2$"**) *background* squares; lay out design as shown. Sew pieces together as indicated trimming 'ears' as you go; remove all basting; press seams open and flat.

This is the basic Amish Friendship Star, a fairly elementary 'nine-patch' design. (What is a nine-patch? - a design made of nine patches!!). Now add some extra textural definition.

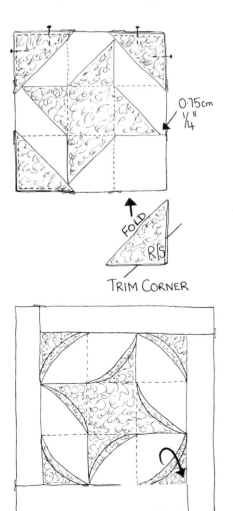

TRIM CORNER

2. Cut four more 12cm (**$4^1/_2$"**) squares in the Star fabric or any other colour. Fold and press all four squares diagonally in half (R/S out) forming triangles. Place one folded square on each corner of the 'nine-patch', aligning all the raw edges. The folded square should touch the tip of the Star. (If you stitched the correct seam width, there will be a 0.75 cm (**$^1/_4$"**) gap on R/S between the tips of the Star and the raw edges of the fabric.) Pin and baste in place. Roll back all the folded edges of all the folded sections and you'll have curves. Wow! Stitch in place.

(Optional: To reduce bulk in the seams trim/cut away part of the back/underside of the folded squares <u>before</u> pinning and basting shape in place. Ensure the cut away portion is <u>underneath/on back</u>. Sew the entire length of the rolled edge down afterwards to prevent the cut portion from fraying.)

Add the border or join to another block before rolling the edges of the outer folded squares, then the rolled back edges will lie on/over the seam and not get trapped in the next seam.

Add even more texture to the design - tuck folded squares into the little pockets or stuff with bits of torn wadding/batting, sew rolled edge in place to prevent the filling or any insert escaping.